nature
ART WORKSHOP

TIPS, TECHNIQUES, AND STEP-BY-STEP PROJECTS FOR CREATING NATURE-INSPIRED ART

Brimming with creative inspiration, how-to projects, and useful information to enrich your everyday life, Quarto Knows is a favorite destination for those pursuing their interests and passions. Visit our site and dig deeper with our books into your area of interest: Quarto Creates, Quarto Cooks, Quarto Homes, Quarto Lives, Quarto Drives, Quarto Explores, Quarto Gifts, or Quarto Kids.

nature
ART WORKSHOP

TABLE OF CONTENTS

Introduction 6

Meet the Artists.. 8

Chapter 1: Flowers 10

Floral Crown 12

Leaf Roses 16

Floral Spiral 20

Sugar Skull 24

How to Press Flowers 28

Pressed-Flower Candle 32

Pressed-Flower Collage............................... 36

Simple Garden Mandala................................ 40

Chapter 2: Stones & Shells 42

Landscape Stone....................................... 44

Hummingbird Stone 46

Star Feather Stone..................................... 50

Seascape Shell... 54

Sunrise Shell... 56

Beach Mandala 60

Negative-Space Heart.................................. 64

Chapter 3: Wood................................66

Log Stamp Artwork................................68

Calligraphy Planters................................70

Painting & Woodburning 72

Painted Wood Slice................................78

Tree Study Wood Slice................................82

Leaf Study Garland................................84

Woodburned Herb Rack 88

Woodburned Constellation Coasters 92

Woodburned Pieces & Color 98

Wooden Wearables................................102

Chapter 4: Other Natural Elements 104

Painted Feather................................106

Painted Acorn................................110

Chapter 5: Nature-Inspired Art................................112

Screen-Printed Pop Art................................114

Golden Moth................................120

Gouache Feather Illustration................................122

Watercolor Raindrops 124

Floral Watercolor................................126

Visit www.quartoknows.com/page/nature-art to download free bonus materials, including artist tips and additional step-by-step projects.

INTRODUCTION

The intricate beauty of nature has inspired artists throughout the ages. From unique textures and vivid color combinations to the beautiful play of light, the natural world is an artist's haven—and there are plenty of new and interesting tools and materials from the natural world to explore! From creating tiny masterpieces on shells, feathers, acorns, and wood slices to artistic arrangements with pressed flowers, leaves, and fresh floral bouquets, all you need for most of the projects in this book can be found in your own backyard.

Nature Art Workshop is about combining your love of art and nature through discovery and creative play. In this book, you will find a wide variety of ideas for making art using materials found in nature, as well as creating artwork inspired by nature. Each step-by-step project features easy-to-follow instructions and colorful images to inspire you to see flowers, rocks, seashells, wood, and other natural elements in new and exciting ways.

MEET THE ARTISTS

Sarah Lorraine Edwards, Sarah Smiles Creations
Fresh Botanical Art

"There is something about taking the natural beauty of the earth and turning it into a piece of artwork that is very charming to me."

Sarah Lorraine Edwards enjoys collaborating with nature for the deep joy and happiness it brings to her life. She holds an art degree from Gonzaga University and has worked in many different art and craft mediums, including drawing, painting, printmaking, sewing, and jewelry making; however, nature art is her favorite. Through this art form, Sarah develops a deeper connection and appreciation for the natural world. She hopes to inspire others to pay closer attention to the life springing forth all around. Visit sarahsmilescreations.com.

Mikko Sumulong, I Try DIY and Mix Fonts
Pressed Flower Art

"Why buy when you can DIY?"

Mikko Sumulong is a crafter, writer, web geek, human resources professional, and a handwritten-font designer. For the last few years, she has been designing fonts, building websites, holding craft events, writing craft books, facilitating workshops, teaching ESL, and doing HR consultant work. She learned the art of pressed botanicals from her mother and has endeavored to share the art form with as many people as possible. Visit itrydiy.me and mixfonts.com.

Katie Brooks, Katie Brooks Art
Painted Shells, Stones & Other Natural Elements

"I gathered a few white seashells during a morning walk. They looked like tiny canvases, and I just had to paint them. I soon began to see tiny canvases everywhere!"

Katie Brooks divides her time between creating and sharing her art and working as a freelance illustrator and designer. She enjoys exploring a range of mediums, including watercolor, acrylic, sculpture, and mixed media, although nature remains her most prevalent inspiration. She paints seashells, pebbles, leaves, acorns, feathers, and everything in between, and incorporates found natural elements into many of her artworks. Visit katiebrooksart.com.

Gabri Joy Kirkendall, Gabri Joy Studios
Gouache and Watercolor Painting

"Gouache lends beautiful contrast to artwork and it is also perfect for adding patterns and details on watercolor."

Artist, author, and illustrator Gabri Joy Kirkendall specializes in hand lettering, watercolor, and pen and ink. Gabri is the artist and owner of Gabri Joy Studios, a successful online business based in the Pacific Northwest that specializes in fine-art prints, invitations, branding, stationery, and more. Visit etsy.com/people/gabrijoy.

Allison Hetzell, By the Rock and Weed
Wood Slice Art

"Creating art that focuses on nature and working with natural materials brings me a lot of joy, especially when I can collect those materials myself."

Allison Hetzell has been running her online shop By the Rock and Weed since 2012, where she sells a small variety of handmade, predominantly nature-themed artwork, often made from natural materials like wood slices and river rocks. Allison loves using a variety of creative materials and methods; however, painting and wood-burning are her two favorites. She always has an eye open for recently fallen tree branches, since she never cuts down living trees for material. Allison loves inspiring people to get out into nature and encapsulate the feelings they have when exploring the wild. Visit www.bytherockandweed.com.

Alix Adams, LitJoy Crate
Home Décor Art

"There are fresh and innovative ways you can add artwork to your décor while staying within a budget."

Alix Adams is the cofounder of LitJoy Crate, a subscription service that offers folks a simple, creative, and easy way to read more—and read more often. LitJoy offers products that create lifelong readers and foster a love of literature. Previously, Alix ran a lifestyle and design blog about crafting a handmade and heartfelt life. Visit litjoycrate.com.

Other Contributors

Chelsea Foy, Lovely Indeed
Screen-printed Pop Art

Chelsea Foy is the blogger behind Lovely Indeed, a creative lifestyle blog with a focus on DIY, travel, family, style, and all the other little things that make life lovely. Visit lovelyindeed.com.

Monica Moody
Woodburned Pieces with Color

Monica Moody is an artist from Dallas, Texas. Known for her vibrant alcohol ink paintings, Monica also enjoys mixed media, illustration, relief printmaking, pyrography, and watercolor painting. Visit www.monicamoody.com to learn more.

Margaret Vance, Ethereal and Earth
Hummingbird Rock Painting

Artist Margaret Vance paints beautifully vibrant and colorful rock art full of intricate detail and pattern. As in nature, no two stones are painted alike. Each stone's size, shape, color, texture, and individuality influence the design to create a singular mix of art and nature. Visit www.etherealandearth.com.

Marisa Redondo, River Luna Art
Star Feather Rock Painting

Artist and illustrator Marissa Redondo works primarily in watercolor and oil. Most of her art is inspired by nature, and art has always been her greatest love. Marisa is fascinated by nature's creations and the little pieces that often go unnoticed, from the fine lines of feathers to the spores of a dandelion. Visit riverlunaart.com.

Alyssa Stokes
Mandalas

Alyssa Stokes is a Baltimore artist and art educator. She is greatly influenced by nature, and her work includes nautical and woodland altered photographs, as well as various still life petal plays.

FLOWERS

Floral Crown

WITH SARAH LORRAINE EDWARDS

When is a great time for a floral crown? Anytime you want to add a bit of magic and majesty to your life! Create floral crowns for weddings, birthdays, anniversaries, baby blessings, or just for fun!

Materials
- Fabric or flexible measuring tape
- 19-gauge floral wire
- Floral tape (green)
- Floral wire cutters
- Greenery
- Flowers, real or faux*

*Note: You can use fresh, faux, or even dried flowers!

1 Measure your head from mid-forehead and over your ears to approximately 1 inch above the hairline on the back of your neck. Add 6 inches and cut two pieces of wire to your measurement. Evenly line up the two wires and begin to wrap the floral tape around the wire at one end. Stretch the tape as you wrap and keep it nice and tight. Continue to wrap the entire length of wire by twisting the wire as you go. As you spiral down the wire, make sure each layer overlaps the previous so no wire is showing.

2 ⤺

Locate the center of the wrapped wire, and measure 6 inches in one direction to locate your starting point. The total area covered in flowers will be about 12 inches. From the starting point, begin to wrap floral tape onto the base wire with the shorter end in front of you. Lay your first stem next to the starting point; then wrap the tape around the stem and wire a few times to secure the flower to the base wire. Remember to stretch with your fingers as you go, keeping the wrap tight. As you work, wrap around each stem a few times around before adding the next piece.

3 ⤺

Continue adding flowers one stem at a time, keeping each new flower close to the previous. Slightly bend the wire as you go to create a curve. Add fewer flowers for a thinner crown, or fill the space in with more flowers for a thicker crown.

4

If you are going for a thicker crown, begin to lessen the thickness of your crown after 6 to 7 inches, adding smaller and smaller pieces toward the end. The total length of the flower section should be about 12 inches long. Use the tape measure along the way to check your progress.

5

When you're done adding flowers, continue to wrap the remaining stems until they are completely covered. Tear or cut the floral tape, and wrap the remaining end around the base. To connect the crown, overlap the two ends by approximately 3 inches. Cut a 2-inch piece of floral tape, and wrap it around the overlapped ends to secure the crown while you try it on. Make adjustments, if needed. When the crown is the size you want it, cut a 12-inch piece of floral tape and completely cover the section where the two ends overlap.

For best appearance, fresh floral crowns should be made right before use, as the flowers will begin to wilt. Try using completely dried flowers to create a floral crown that will last many years! There are a few types of flowers that keep their shape and color when dried, such as strawflowers, statice, and celosia. Dried seed pods, such as poppy and paper moon, also make great additions to a dried flower crown.

To help your crown last longer, spray a coat or two of non-yellowing clear acrylic gloss over the entire piece and hang outside or in a well-ventilated area for a few days.

Leaf Roses

WITH SARAH LORRAINE EDWARDS

Leaf roses are a wonderful way to preserve the beauty of autumn. They can be displayed alone in a vase, or you can make a variety of roses to create an entire bouquet. These pretty leaf roses make great autumn gifts or decorations and are perfect for a Thanksgiving centerpiece or a fall wedding.

Materials
- 10 to 20 autumn leaves per rose
- Floral wire or small, sturdy twig
- Floral tape (brown or green)
- Non-yellowing clear acrylic gloss spray

Use leaves that are soft and pliable. If they crack when you fold them, they won't work for this project.

1

Start with smaller leaves and increase the leaf size as you go. Begin by folding the first leaf in half so the tip and stem are next to each other, with the colorful side out. Leaves with stems still attached will create a sturdier, longer-lasting rose. Roll the folded leaf from one side, keeping the folded edge on top.

2

Keeping the first rolled leaf in one hand, fold your next leaf in half. Roll the second leaf around the first.

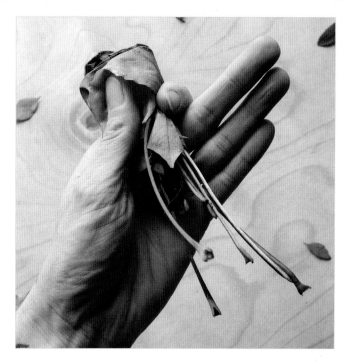

3

Continue adding leaves in this same way, turning the rose as you go to maintain an even size. You can create roses of all one color or multicolored roses.

4

Continue holding the rose in one hand as you add more leaves. If you set it down, the rose it will unravel and you'll have to start over.

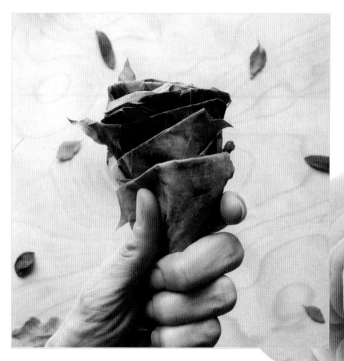

5

If the center of the rose begins to poke up too far, gently push it back down. You may need to do this a few times as you go.

6

As you near completion of the rose, start tapering the leaf layers downward. This will help hold all the layers in. Use the largest leaves at the bottom, and stop adding leaves when you're happy with the size.

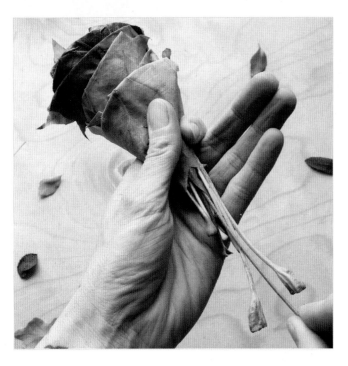

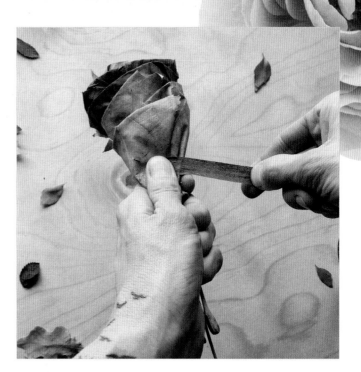

7

Gently slide a 9- or 10-inch piece of floral wire into the rose as far as possible without upsetting the layers. You could also use a small, sturdy twig.

8

Holding the rose in one hand, place the end of the floral tape under your thumb, and turn the rose gently to wrap the tape around the base, stretching the tape as you go to keep it as tight as possible.

9

Wrap seven to ten layers of tape around the base.

10

Continue wrapping down the wire and stems until you reach the end of the wire. Cover the end in tape, and wrap back up the stem slightly. Tear the tape off when you are done.

After the roses have had a few days to dry, spray them with non-yellowing clear acrylic gloss to help lock in color and preserve them longer.

Floral Spiral

WITH SARAH LORRAINE EDWARDS

Watching plants change throughout the seasons, I have discovered the many phases they go through—from seed to full-grown plant and back to seed again. I began to view the process as a spiral, rather than a circle, because the plants never return to the exact same spot, but rather continue on in a life spiral.

Materials
- Natural objects (rocks, shells, crystals, flowers, etc.)
- Scissors

1 Gather pieces of nature from your yard or public nature areas. Starting in the middle of your design area, begin arranging the items. I like to start with smaller pieces in the center and gradually use larger ones as I work outward. Place one item after the next, creating a curve around the starting point.

If you're unable to gather your own items, you can purchase a bouquet of flowers from a local market or find natural items at a craft supply store.

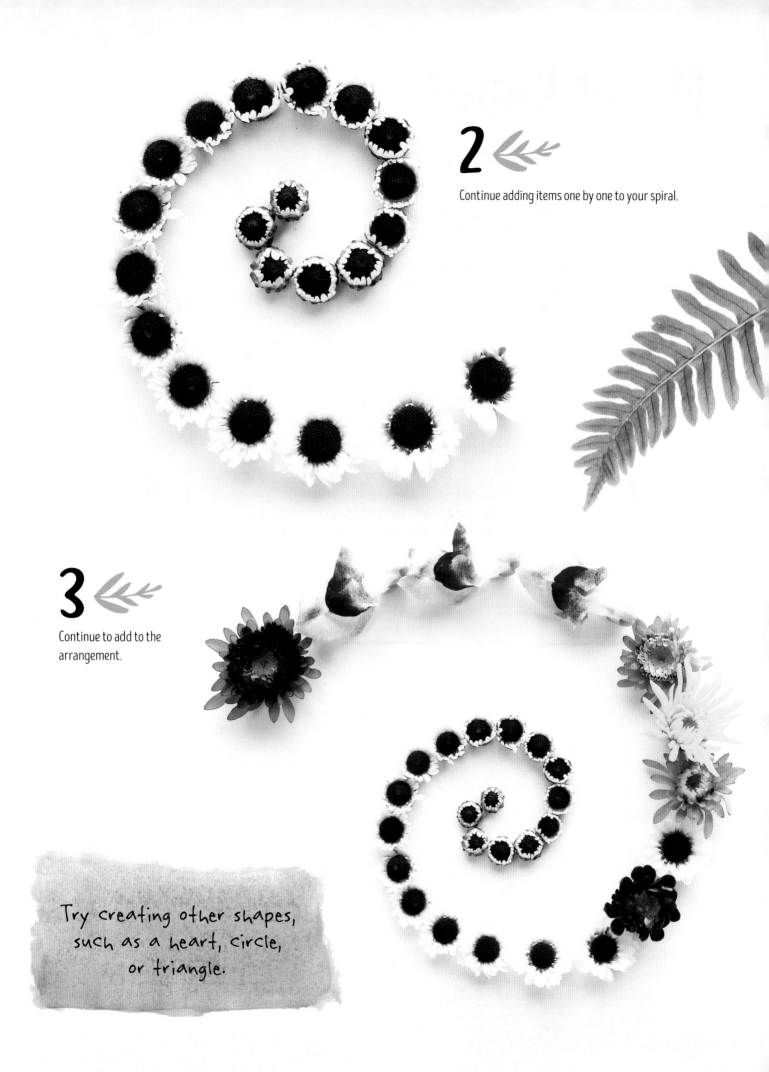

2

Continue adding items one by one to your spiral.

3

Continue to add to the arrangement.

Try creating other shapes, such as a heart, circle, or triangle.

4

Keep adding nature items until you're happy with the spiral. I add a little tail of petals to the end of mine.

5

Embellish the spiral with more nature items, if desired. I add little petals around some of the flowers. You can add as many as you like until you feel your spiral is complete.

6 Take a photo of your spiral to create a lasting memory of your artwork that you can share with others.

Sugar Skull

WITH SARAH LORRAINE EDWARDS

Sugar skulls are common during the *Día de los Muertos*, or Day of the Dead, celebration. They are always colorful to reflect the vibrancy of life. Creating a sugar skull design from flowers and plants could be a way to honor someone who has passed, or it can simply be an enjoyable project. Begin by gathering pieces of nature, such as flowers, leaves, rocks, sticks, and shells. Find a workspace on the ground, a desk or table, or even the floor.

Materials
- Natural materials (fresh flowers, leaves, rocks, sticks, shells, etc.)
- Large sheet of paper or wood (optional)
- Scissors

1

Gather your materials. Choose two similar pieces for the eyes. The eyes are the central focus, so be sure to choose pieces that will stand out and aren't too small. Select two large petals or small leaves for the nose. Then cut a stem for the line of the mouth. Leave enough space to place teeth above the line.

2

Choose petals or leaves for the teeth. Cut the tips of the petals off, making some larger than others. Start by adding two teeth at the top center. Continue adding petals on either side to fill in the line. Then add petal teeth to the bottom of the line. I use the front of the petals for the top and the back of the petals for the bottom to create contrast.

Use a stem to help move pieces into place. Sometimes this works better than your fingers!

3

As you continue, choose pairs of flowers or plants that are similar in size to add to each side. To begin the outer design of the skull, pick two pieces to represent the cheeks. Place these on either side of the nose, just outside the eyes. Then use stems, or small flowers with stems, at either side of the mouth.

4

Continue adding flowers, stems, and leaves two at a time, one on each side of the skull, directly across from each other.

5

Use slightly curved pieces to complete the chin and top of the head. I like to finish the skull with a flower at the very center of the top and bottom of the design.

6

You may also like to add two petals for rosy cheeks. Feel free to add leaf or petal embellishments to the forehead, chin, or other areas.

7 Play around until you have a design you like. You can stop here, or sprinkle small petals around the background for a different effect. I use mostly white petals with a few purple petals for contrast. Take a few photos of your creation to print and frame.

How to Press Flowers

WITH MIKKO SUMULONG

Pressing flowers is the natural craft of preserving blooms as they are, extending their life by weeks, months, or even years! You don't need many supplies to create your own pressed floral art. You don't even need a real flower press, although it's nice to have. Here are the materials I recommend for collecting, pressing, and preserving fresh botanicals.

Cutting & Gathering

While collecting botanicals, you'll need cutting implements to clean off debris or trim unusable parts. Take plastic zip bags and paper towels with you to collect fresh botanicals for pressing. Don't limit yourself to "perfect" flowers and foliage. Imperfect presses still make for really interesting masterpieces.

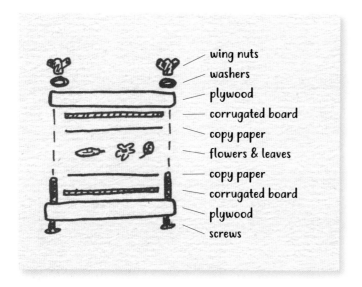

- wing nuts
- washers
- plywood
- corrugated board
- copy paper
- flowers & leaves
- copy paper
- corrugated board
- plywood
- screws

Pressing

To press fresh botanicals, you'll need heavy books, weights (optional), and plain copy paper. You can also make your own flower press with pieces of plywood and some clamps or screws. Keep in mind that not all flowers retain their color. Some flowers on the scarlet-purple side retain a dark crimson color. Paler petals may turn brown. Grass, weeds, and vines tend to keep their original color.

Handling & Crafting

Use handmade paper or card stock, craft glue, and paintbrushes to create artwork with your pressed flowers. Avoid handling pressed items with your fingers. Instead, use a palette knife, spatula, Popsicle stick, or butter knife. Touching pressed flowers may transfer oils from your fingers to the piece, which could invite mold and mildew later.

1 Gather your favorite botanicals. It's best to harvest your picks on a sunny afternoon, so that any morning dew has dried. Avoid flowers with pods, pistils, and pollen. These types of flowers are easily attacked by mildew. Store what you pick in plastic zip bags with a bit of air for a day or two before pressing. The same goes for bouquets. Be sure to take the bouquet out of water for at least a day before pressing.

2 Make sure that the flowers and leaves are free from any moisture and bugs. Remove any hard or bulky seed cases, calyxes, or stems. It's always best to break flowers down to the most basic parts. For instance, it's wise to press petals, instead of an entire bud all together.

3 Press your petals, blooms, and leaves between two sheets of copy paper inside a heavy book. The copy paper will absorb any excess moisture in the flowers. Lay the flowers facedown to avoid folds or tears, and space the pieces out so they don't dry and stick together. Group flowers and leaves of the same type and thickness together. Label and date each press for quick and easy tracking.

4 Close the pages of your books, and store in a cool dry place. Stack books on top of each other, or place weights on top for added weight and even pressing. Then put your patience to the test. Leave the presses alone for 6 to 8 weeks. Do your best not to introduce moisture back to the flowers—you're not allowed to peek!

5  After the recommended pressing period, check if the presses are ready. A quick test is to pick up a flower by the tip. If the flower is floppy, it is not yet fully dried and pressed. If the flower is stiff, you can start using it for your projects.

6  If you're not yet ready to use pressed flowers, it's best to store and repackage them. Carefully transfer the pieces into plastic zip bags, housed in envelopes or folded sheets of copy paper.

Pressed-Flower Candle

WITH MIKKO SUMULONG

Spruce up a plain candle by adding pressed leaves or flowers to it. Custom and one-of-a-kind, this decorated piece is bound to spark conversations!

Materials
- Smooth wax candle
- Copy paper
- Lighter or second candle
- Old metal spoon
- Pressed flowers and leaves

1

Cut a strip of paper the same height as your candle, and use it to plan your design. Select your pressed materials carefully. If you're using a cylindrical candle, make sure brittle pieces won't break when they are placed on the candle.

2

Light a separate candle as a heat source. Hold an old metal spoon over the flame. Get it just warm enough to melt the wax. Be careful—the spoon can get hot quickly!

3

Hover the spoon over your candle. Warm a spot on the candle just long enough for the surface to soften, without letting the wax come to a drip.

4

Place a flower or leaf over the melted spot. The wax acts as glue. Don't worry if it doesn't stick right away!

The spoon might start to collect soot from the flame. If this happens, carefully wipe the dark spots off the spoon, so that it doesn't transfer onto the candle. Be careful not to burn yourself if the spoon is still hot!

5 Smoothly glide the spoon over the leaf or flower to coat it with more wax to help seal it in.

6 Reheat the spoon as needed, and repeat until all the flowers and leaves are placed on the candle. Display along with other pressed flower pieces for a beautiful nature-themed mantle or shelf at home!

Pressed-Flower Collage

WITH MIKKO SUMULONG

One of the best ways to show off your pressed flowers is by making fun and colorful wall art.

Materials
- Copy paper
- Card stock
- Pencil
- Stylus (optional)
- Pressed flowers, leaves, and stems
- Glue
- Paintbrush

1  Sketch out your chosen shape on a plain sheet of copy paper—consider animals, objects, or perhaps silhouettes of your kids. Make sure to accentuate or exaggerate any distinct features. This will make the finished piece more striking.

2

Mark the center of the finished sketch. Align the center of the sketch with the center of the card stock for your actual collage piece. Once everything is aligned, trace over your design with a dull pencil or a stylus. This will leave score marks on the card stock, giving you a faint outline of the sketch, without the trouble of having to erase pencil marks later.

3

Start picking out flowers, leaves, and stems from your pressed botanicals collection. Plan your design on a clean sheet of paper for visual approval. It's best to start with the outline of the shape, and work your way inward. Fill the space as best as you can, using an assortment of colors, shapes, and textures.

4 «

Using a brush, apply a very thin coat of glue on the reverse side of each flower or leaf. Make sure to cover the strategic areas first, including the spine, stem, and thicker parts.

5 «

Carefully apply each piece to the card stock. If needed, use a toothpick to straighten out any folded areas or burst any bubbles that may have formed. Remember to be very gentle! Allow to dry; then check for loose pieces by gently blowing on the flowers.

6 Take a step back and see if everything looks the way you want it. On the back, you may want to note all the flowers you used for identification in the future. Frame your artwork, and display in your home or give it as a gift.

Simple Garden Mandala

WITH ALYSSA STOKES

This easy-to-create garden mandala uses common weeds and wildflowers to create a sweet pastel design. It's a great mandala for beginners, and you can also repeat and build upon it to create more complex designs.

Materials
- Cut flowers
- Clover plant
- Small round objects
- Scissors
- Tweezers
- Color paint swatches (optional)

1 Trim your flowers and clover plant, separating each petal and leaf. Select a limited color palette, such as the pink and green that you see here. For the small round objects, I am using pink chocolate-covered sunflower seeds. You could use other types of small candies, buttons, stones, or beads.

2 Arrange four or five petals in a circular shape. Place the inside part of the flower, pistil, stamen, or other round object in the middle of the circle.

3 Select several clover leaves that are about the same size. Place them next to each petal, and use your tweezers to adjust the small leaves so that they face outward.

Place small round objects or other flower parts in the spaces between each leaf. If you like, complement your simple mandala by placing paint swatches in similar colors next to or behind your design.

After photographing and editing your mandala, try making your own greeting cards by printing the image on card stock.

STONES & SHELLS

Landscape Stone

WITH KATIE BROOKS

Stones are easily accessible and affordable, making them the perfect surface for some nature-inspired artwork. Smooth, flat stones are ideal, but you can also create interesting artwork on stones with more texture or irregularities. If you don't live near a place where you can collect stones in nature, you can purchase them from craft stores, garden centers, or even online.

Materials
- Stones
- Craft paints
- Matte varnish
- Paintbrushes
- Paint palette

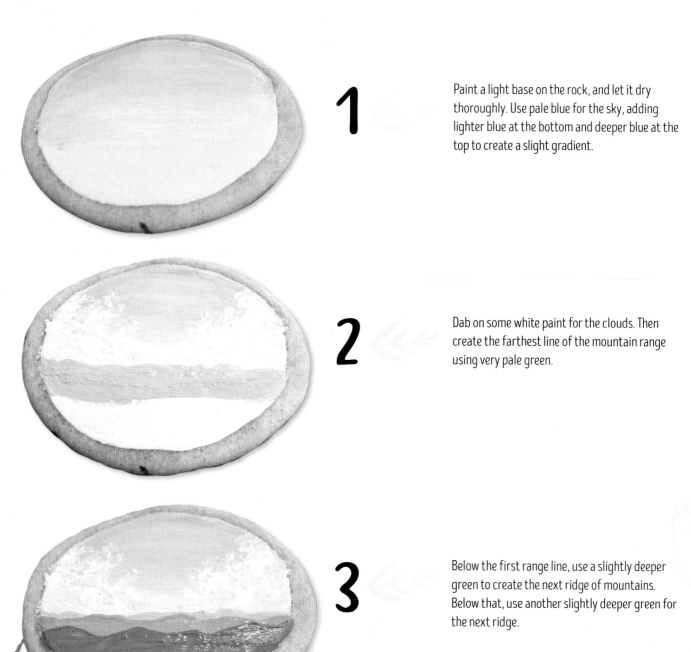

1 Paint a light base on the rock, and let it dry thoroughly. Use pale blue for the sky, adding lighter blue at the bottom and deeper blue at the top to create a slight gradient.

2 Dab on some white paint for the clouds. Then create the farthest line of the mountain range using very pale green.

3 Below the first range line, use a slightly deeper green to create the next ridge of mountains. Below that, use another slightly deeper green for the next ridge.

Unless you're painting a very light-colored rock, a light base coat of paint creates the perfect blank canvas for your artwork.

4 Add one more dark green ridge at the bottom. The gradation of color creates the effect of atmospheric perspective, suggesting distance.

5 Now, using your darkest green, paint vertical lines of varying heights at the bottom of the image and create the foliage on each tree, working on one side at a time and tapering toward the top.

6 Seal over with matte varnish, and you're finished!

Hummingbird Stone

WITH MARGARET VANCE

Hummingbirds are one of my favorite creatures. Happily darting about the garden, they are flying jewels of joy. Their varied colors make hummingbirds the perfect subject for rock art.

Materials
- Stones
- Craft paints
- Matte varnish
- Paintbrushes
- Paint palette

1

Choose a flat, smooth rock with a shape you like. Remove any dirt from the rock and ensure that it is completely dry. The rock's shape, size, texture, and color can guide your color and design choices.

2

Start by creating the head and body placement of the hummingbird. I like to use similar colors for the body and head to help distinguish the outline of the hummingbird, and then use a variety of different but similar hues for the wings and tail feathers.

3

Next add wings to the back of the body and tail feathers to the bottom.

4

When the paint on the hummingbird's head is completely dry, and you are satisfied with the color tones, use black paint to place the eye and a long beak extending from the head.

5 Next create the hummingbird's garden using flowers, mandalas, sun images, and other natural elements. Remember to let each section of paint dry completely before handling the rock.

6 Once your rock is finished and the paint is dry, use an all-purpose clear lacquer spray to protect and seal your finished stone.

Star Feather Stone

WITH MARISA REDONDO

This simple stone design reminds us of the intricate beauty of nature that often goes unnoticed, from the smallest snowflake to the softest feather.

Materials
- Stones
- Craft paints
- Matte varnish
- Paintbrushes
- Paint palette

1 Apply a thin and even layer of varnish to your rock. Once the varnish is dry, begin by painting a thin line centered on your rock with a small round paintbrush.

2 Paint a feather tuft outline around the centerline.

3  Paint V-shaped lines to divide the feather into sections.

4 Fill the tip of your feather with fine lines.

5

Create a triangular shape within the feather by painting two lines in each section.

6

Fill the area outside the triangles with fine, feather-like lines.

7

Add dots to the triangle border.

8 🌿 Lastly, paint a tiny star in each of the triangles. When your painting is finished, allow it to dry completely. Apply a thin layer of sealing varnish. Let dry, and add one more thin coat of varnish.

Seascape Shell

WITH KATIE BROOKS

Painted shells are easier to make than you think—and they are the perfect way to commemorate a special trip. I recommend gathering them along the beach yourself, as allowed by your local municipality, as gift shops often have questionable methods of collecting shells. Finding your natural canvas yourself is not only more sustainable, but far more memorable!

Materials
- Seashell
- Craft paints
- Matte varnish (optional)
- Paintbrushes (round brushes with a strong point are ideal)
- Paint palette

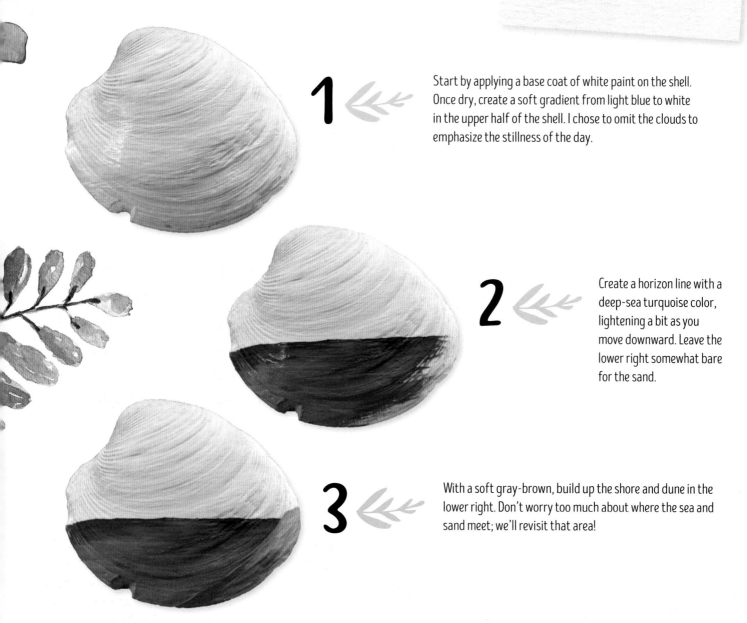

1 Start by applying a base coat of white paint on the shell. Once dry, create a soft gradient from light blue to white in the upper half of the shell. I chose to omit the clouds to emphasize the stillness of the day.

2 Create a horizon line with a deep-sea turquoise color, lightening a bit as you move downward. Leave the lower right somewhat bare for the sand.

3 With a soft gray-brown, build up the shore and dune in the lower right. Don't worry too much about where the sea and sand meet; we'll revisit that area!

Always begin by coating the shell with white paint. Shells come in a range of colors, and their coloration may affect the paint's appearance without a base coat.

4 Using a light tint of turquoise, suggest cresting waves at the shoreline and in smaller proportion as they move backward in the scene.

5 Using your smallest brush and a touch of white paint, emphasize the sea-foam along the waves, especially where they meet the sand.

When visiting the beach, I like to make a tradition of painting at least one shell to leave behind on the shore. What a nice surprise for someone to find!

6 With the same tiny brush, paint slight upward strokes at the top of the dune in varying shades of green to create seagrass. Add a small flock of seagulls; then seal your finished painting with matte varnish.

Sunrise Shell

WITH KATIE BROOKS

This painting was inspired by a morning walk along the beach at sunrise. Preserving a memory on a seashell makes for a wonderfully unique souvenir!

Materials
- Seashell
- Craft paints
- Matte varnish (optional)
- Paintbrushes
- Paint palette

1

Apply a layer of white paint over the whole shell to create a base layer for your painting. Allow to dry. Create a soft gradient from pale blue to pale yellow. I find it works best to create a blue-to-white gradient first and let it dry before adding pale yellow—this way, you avoid a green sky!

2

Continue the gradient from pale yellow to orange, coral, and faded purple. Use this line of purple to mark the horizon.

3 ✦

Introduce a lavender-tinted blue beneath the horizon line to block out the ocean. Be sure to create the shape of overlapping waves along the shore!

4 ✦

Using the colors from the sunrise, begin accenting the water with reflections from the sky. Work from darkest to lightest to create the strongest highlights.

5

Along the waves, place a strip of orange and yellow down the shore.

6

Block in the sand in the remaining white space. Use dark gray, to allow the sunrise to steal the show!

7

Using the purple and coral from the sunrise, create loose, fluffy clouds in the sky. You may want to add small yellow accents at the bottom to capture the light.

8

Time for details! Using your smallest brush, lightly speckle white along the crest of the waves to imply sea-foam. I also use watered down white paint to lightly brush in rays from the sun. Add a tiny flock of birds. Seal your finished painting with varnish.

Beach Mandala

WITH ALYSSA STOKES

This nature mandala is perfect for a summer trip to the beach, but you can create it any time of year using your shell collection and a little gathered sand.

Materials
- Shells
- Beach stones
- Sand

1

Organize your shells and stones, arranging the items by size and color. I grouped my shells into five sets of three, with three of the same general type, size, and color. Select a few more stones, 6 or 12 in a set, to fill in the mandala design.

2 ⋘

Pour and pat the sand into a thin layer. Work on a large sheet of white paper for easy cleanup! Create a natural looking edge to the sand by gradually thinning it out.

3 ⋘

Select one unique shell for the focal point, and place it in the center of the sand circle. Then begin with two smaller shell sets. Arrange the shells evenly around the central focal point, alternating between the two types.

4

Continue to work out radially from the center point, by placing the next two sets of shells. Line up the outer shells with the inner ring of shells previously placed.

5

Place six of one type of stone between each shell in the inner ring. Then repeat this for the outer ring, using a different set of stones. If you wish, add more shells or stones to the outer ring of the mandala.

The beach mandala makes a great summer-themed centerpiece for a table!

Negative-Space Heart

WITH SARAH LORRAINE EDWARDS

Playing with nature is fun and relaxing. I continue to add to my collection of treasures, which includes rocks, shells, beach glass, and even crystals.

Materials
- Paper
- Pencil
- Scissors
- Natural objects (rocks, shells, crystals, flowers, etc.)

1

Draw or print your chosen shape and cut it out. Choose a surface to work on. This could be a table, desk, piece of wood, or paper. (I'm using a piece of wood painted black.) Place your shape in the center of the workspace, and use a rock to hold it in place. Surround the edge of the shape with pieces of nature, such as rocks, shells, and crystals.

2

Once you've fully surrounded the shape, continue to add new items. For me, this process is like putting together a puzzle. You may end up moving a piece around until you find the perfect spot.

3

Continue adding items, incorporating a few that are extra unique to add visual interest and texture. Continue to add elements until you feel the project is complete.

4

When you're done adding items, carefully remove the paper from the center. Adjust any pieces, if necessary, and take a photo if you like. You may not want to take a photo at all. Nature art is often referred to as being ephemeral—a fleeting, transitory moment. These creations are mostly for your own enjoyment, so have fun with it!

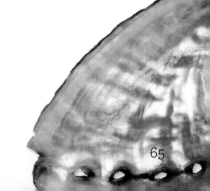

WOOD

Log Stamp Artwork

WITH ALIX ADAMS

Purchasing artwork for your home can be expensive. Luckily, there are fresh, innovative, and inexpensive ways to create artwork for your home. This log stamp artwork is interesting, simple to make, and easily customizable.

Materials
- Card stock or art-grade paper
- Acrylic craft paints
- Foam craft brushes
- Log slices or log cross sections*
- Picture frame

*I cut some scrap wood using a miter saw and then sanded the surfaces smooth.

1

Choose a log slice for your first stamp. I enjoy using a variety of log slice shapes and sizes because it adds interest to the artwork. Using a foam brush, cover the face of the log slice in a coat of paint. The more paint you apply, the more brilliant and bold the stamp mark will be.

2

Next, while the paint is still wet, carefully stamp the log slice on the art paper. Once you place the painted surface on the paper, press firmly on the log slice to ensure a solid stamp impression.

3 ≪≪

Repeat, stamping with the other log slices in various colors to create a dynamic pattern. I like the stamp marks to have varying coverage, so I covered some logs in thicker layers of paint and some in thinner layers before stamping.

4 ≪≪

Allow the paint to dry completely; then frame!

Calligraphy Planters

WITH ALIX ADAMS

These simple wooden planters are transformed into something unique and special with the use of paint markers and a little calligraphy practice. They are so simple to make and easy to love!

Materials
- Paint markers in colors of your choice
- Pots or planter boxes*

*Paint markers can write on terra-cotta, glass, plastic, or wood.

1 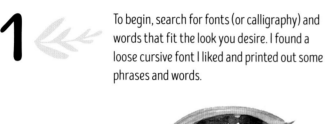 To begin, search for fonts (or calligraphy) and words that fit the look you desire. I found a loose cursive font I liked and printed out some phrases and words.

2 Coax the paint to the tip of the pen by pushing the tip down on a piece of scrap paper several times. Once the paint has filled up the tip, practice writing some words on scrap paper until you are comfortable with the feel of the pen.

3

Carefully write the word or phrase on the planter with the paint pen. Be careful not to smear the word as you write.

4

Once the paint dries, your planters are complete and ready to liven up any living space or patio!

Painting & Woodburning

WITH ALLISON HETZELL

Everyone has a different way of working, and not all techniques will work the same for every person. But the best way of learning is to try it yourself! Here are some introductory tools, tips, and techniques that I use to get you started with wood slice art.

Tools & Materials

Wood Slices

The two best types of wood slices that I have found for painting and woodburning are basswood and birch, which are also the types most likely to be sold in your local craft store. They are softer woods, which makes woodburning far easier, and they're also very light in color, so your artwork is clearly visible.

Woodburning Tools

There are two main types of woodburners: single-temperature and variable-temperature. Different systems may have additional features, but all of them are, in some part, electric, pen-like tools that are heated to create burns in wood with a variety of tips.

- Single-temperature woodburners are solitary pen systems with interchangeable, screw-in tips that heat to a preset level. These are usually the more affordable woodburners that you can purchase in most craft stores, and are great beginner systems.

- Variable temperature woodburners are more expensive, but the cost is worth it if you want to do a considerable amount of woodburning—especially more detailed work. They have quicker heating and cooling times, an adjustable temperature to fit the work you are doing, and a wider variety of tips to choose from.

Single-temperature woodburner (left) and variable-temperature woodburner (right)

Additional Tools

Additional tools for drawing and planning your artwork include:

• Sandpaper and sanding blocks (a foam core surrounded with sanding material) are great for smoothing your pieces and doing touch-up work on woodburnings. Use finer-grit sanding material, like 220 or 320, as coarser grits can leave visible scratches in your work.

• Craft or hobby knives are extremely useful for scraping off mistakes made with a woodburner and they are more precise than sandpaper.

• Pencils for sketching. Use a softer and lighter lead, like 2B or 4B, that can be easily removed and won't leave indentations in the wood.

• An eraser. I have found that the best kind to use on wood is a kneaded rubber eraser. This is a gray, malleable eraser that you can press down onto pencil marks to remove, without leaving markings or little pieces of eraser behind.

• Spray-on acrylic sealers are a great and easy way to finish and protect painted wood pieces, and they are usually available in various matte and gloss versions.

• Polyurethane is a brush-on sealer available in gloss, semi-gloss, matte, and satin versions.

Painting Tools

Acrylic paints are a great way to add opaque colors to wood slices. If you prefer a more muted color wash or want the woodgrain to show through, watercolor paints also work well.

Because painting on wood can be rough on paintbrushes, I usually keep an array of inexpensive brushes on hand in different types and sizes.

Here are some other helpful items to have on hand when working with wood:
- Ruler
- Drill
- Small screwdriver or pliers for changing tips on woodburners
- Paper towels and water for cleanup
- Painter's tape
- Hanging materials (e.g. sawtooth hangers and hemp cord)
- Gesso paint for creating a smoother painting surface

Painting on Wood

I always start wood-slice paintings by making sure they are sanded smooth—the smoother they are, the easier to paint! If your wood slice has some porous areas or dark knots that you would rather not show through your final painting, add a layer or two of white, acrylic gesso paint before getting started. It's a great base to build your artwork on—especially because certain woods absorb a lot of paint; a base layer really helps build more opaque colors.

Paintbrush types from top to bottom: round, flat, liner, filbert

Brush Tips for Painting Nature

I tend to use inexpensive paintbrushes, because wood can be more damaging to a brush than canvas or paper. While I like to have a wide variety on hand, these are the main types that I use for painting on wood:

• **Round:** The round or pointed tip is good for creating thin-to-thick lines and for outlining.

• **Flat:** This brush is ideal for filling in larger areas and creating smooth, straight edges and lines.

• **Liner:** The liner is perfect for drawing thin lines, outlines, and smaller details.

• **Filbert:** This brush is ideal for blending colors, as well as creating round edges and filling larger areas. It's also a good brush for creating leafy trees and bushes—just use a little paint and repeatedly dab the upright paintbrush onto the wood.

Woodburning

There is a wide variety of woodburning tips available to fit your needs, and most can be used in multiple ways to achieve different effects. Regardless of which woodburner you choose, I recommend you at least have one tip for shading, one for writing, and another for thinner line work. Pen tips may differ by the type of woodburner you choose, but shown here are a few examples of frequently used tips.

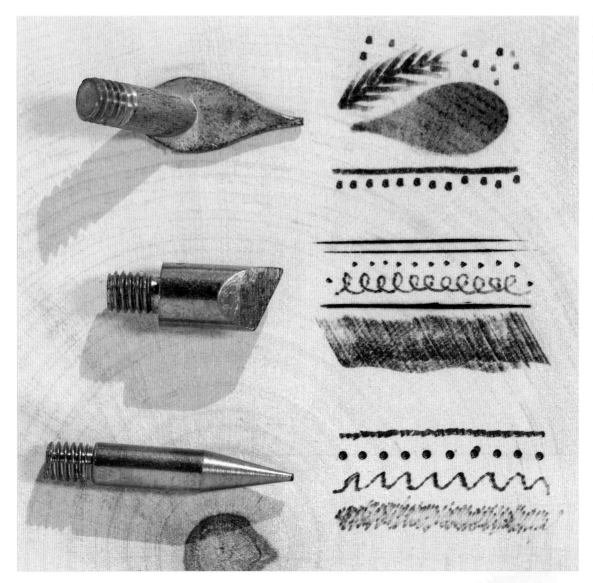

Single-temperature woodburner tips from top to bottom: shading, universal, tapered point

Single-Temperature Woodburner

- **Shading:** The shading tip is great for darkening larger areas, as well as for shading.

- **Universal or Chisel:** This tip, with its tapered chisel shape, is ideal for line work and finer detail, especially if you tilt it to use one of the chisel's points.

- **Tapered Point:** This tip works well as a general drawing tip, as well as for writing and dots.

Keep a piece of scrap wood nearby for practicing techniques, experimenting with different tips, and testing the heat of your woodburning tool.

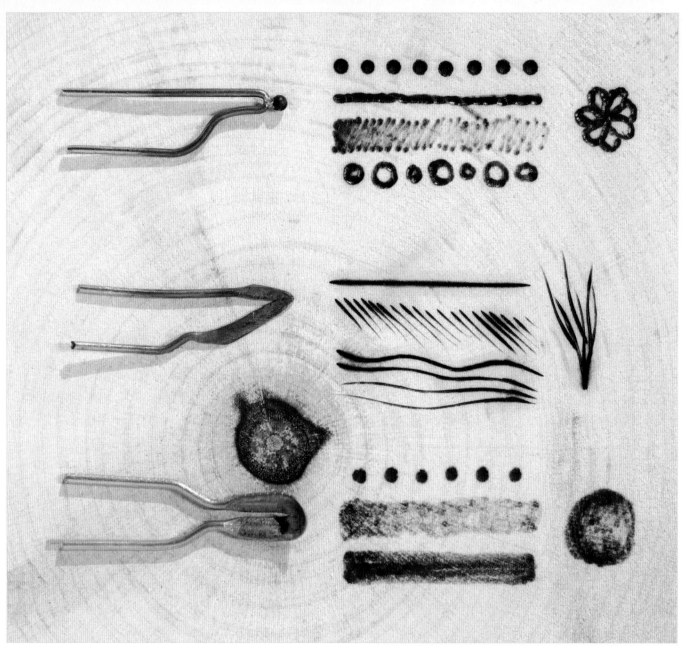

Variable-temperature woodburner tips from top to bottom: ballpoint, round knife, spoon shader

These are just a few of the options available. When choosing your woodburner, research what types of tips are available, what tips it may come with, and which are recommended as the most useful. You may even find additional uses for some tips with practice!

Variable-Temperature Woodburner

- **Ballpoint:** Although there are specific "writing" tips, I often use a very small ballpoint tip to write with my woodburner. This tip is also great for outlining, general drawing, and dots.
- **Round Knife:** The round knife is one of my favorites; it's great for creating very thin lines and feathering, and its rounded tip makes drawing curves fairly easy.
- **Spoon Shader:** This is an excellent shading tip. Its larger surface area curves up like a spoon, so the tip's edges do not show up in the burning.

Using the Woodburner

- Once you select and securely attach the tip you would like to use, turn on your woodburner and give it the recommended time to preheat. I like to test the heated tip on scrap wood first so I know how quickly it burns and what shape the tip will create.

- The darkness of the burn depends largely on how quickly you drag the tip across the wood. Moving slowly allows the burner to reheat while you move it, whereas moving quickly uses most of the heat at the start to create a darker burn that fades out as you move. If you let the tip sit in one spot too long it will leave a darker and deeper mark. If you notice your lines getting too light, your burner needs to reheat, so just lift the tip off the wood for a few moments. You can always go back and darken an area, but it's difficult to remove a darker burn.

- Let the woodburner do the work—don't apply too much pressure, or you will burn too deep into the wood or damage your pen tips.

Taking Care of Your Woodburner

To keep your tips in good shape, periodically sand them with fine-grit sandpaper or a nail file—you can even use a craft knife to scrape off some of the carbon buildup.

Precautions

- Keep your woodburner turned off whenever it's not in use, or when you are changing or cleaning pen tips.
- Never burn wood that has been sealed with polyurethane or otherwise treated—the fumes created by burning treated wood are toxic.
- Certain woods or heat levels can create a bit of smoke that may irritate your eyes. Keep your wood tilted on a sloped surface while working to avoid this.

Removing Scorch Marks

The hotter your woodburner is, the more likely it is to leave dark yellow scorch marks around the area you are working on. To lighten or remove these, use a bit of fine-grit sandpaper on the area, or carefully scrape the wood with a craft knife for more precise removal.

Sealing Your Wood

It's important to protect your finished wood pieces from things like moisture, dust, and sunlight. There are several options, and it comes down to personal preference, but I most often use acrylic spray sealer or polyurethane. Acrylic spray sealer is an easy and effective finish that should not cause your piece to yellow; it's available in a variety of matte and glossy options.

Polyurethane is a brush-on sealer available in satin, matte, semi-gloss, and gloss versions. Read the instructions carefully; some can yellow your overall piece, which may look nice on a plain woodburning but interferes with colors if you have done any painting. Search for a non-yellowing, water-based polyurethane if you want to keep your original colors. The first layer or two will soak into the wood, so I usually apply three or four layers.

You can also try different stains and oil-based finishes—just keep in mind that an oil-based finish should not be used on acrylic paints, and these finishes will almost certainly affect the coloring of your piece. With any of these sealers and finishes, always apply them outside or in a well-ventilated area so you do not inhale the fumes.

Painted Wood Slice

WITH ALLISON HETZELL

There are so many beautiful and memorable landscapes that pass through our lives—from favorite childhood haunts and family vacations to a special tree we like to watch change with the seasons. Commemorate your favorite natural landscape with this project—or find a whole new view on a nature walk with your camera!

Materials
• Wood slice
• Landscape photo
• Pencil
• Painter's tape
• Acrylic paint
• Paint palette
• Various paintbrushes
• Water and paper towel
• Acrylic sealer
• Drill
• Hemp cord or twine

1

Use a photo of a landscape with a simply shaped object, such as a tree or mountain range, that takes up a good portion of the photo. Then, breaking the photo down into sections, sketch the landscape onto a wood slice with a pencil. Keep in mind that the closer something is to you, the larger and more detailed it appears.

2

Cover the largest object—in this case, the tree trunk—with painter's tape. After everything is painted, you'll peel this off to reveal the woodgrain. You may need to cut the tape to fit the shape. Be sure to press it down firmly.

3

Set up your paint palette with as many colors as you think you'll need, and keep a glass of water and paper towel handy for cleaning your brush. Then start with a base layer of paint, covering the various sections of the painting with their most dominant color. You can also do some basic shading at this point to help build up the scene.

4

Once the base layer is dry, begin adding detail, starting with the area farthest away in the landscape—usually the sky. Objects become increasingly detailed the closer they are to the foreground. Remember to pay attention to the angle of the sun, noting which sides of objects are in shadow and which are brighter.

5

Once the paint is fully dry, carefully peel up the painter's tape. You may want to score the edge of the tape with a blade before removing it to prevent paint from peeling up.

6 Touch up the edges left behind by the tape. You can blend in the blank area by adding extra little details that might be in front of the object, such as loose branches or flowers.

7 When the painting is finished, apply a coating of acrylic sealer over the wood slice. This will also help enhance the colors of both the wood and your painting. Once the sealer is dry, drill a hole into the top, making sure to drill through the wood and not the bark, which could break off. Finally, thread some twine or hemp cord through the hole and knot it so the piece is ready for hanging!

If you'd rather not drill a hole into your piece, set it up on a small easel.

Tree Study Wood Slice

WITH ALLISON HETZELL

Enjoy a nature walk while searching for inspiration and natural trinkets like nutshells and pine cones to make this beautiful wall hanging!

Materials
- Wood slice (around 8" long)
- Nature finds (pine cones, acorns, feathers, shells, etc.)
- Tree photo or sketch
- Pencil
- Drill
- Acrylic paint
- Paint palette
- Various paintbrushes
- Water and paper towel
- Acrylic sealer

1

On your wood slice, measure out seven spaces about ½-inch apart at the bottom, starting with the space at the center and working out to either side. Mark these spots with a pencil, along with the spot at the top center of your slice where you will string some cord for hanging. Then use a drill to make a hole in each of these marked spots. Be sure to drill into the wood slice and not the bark, which can break off.

2

Sketch a tree onto your wood slice in pencil. Consider what shape best fits the wood slice. Tree branches start large near the trunk and taper off near the ends, with smaller branches splitting off. Don't worry about making the upper portion too detailed—you'll be painting over a lot of it with foliage. Add some winding roots that reach out of the trunk and connect to the drilled holes.

3 Fill in the tree shape with brown paint. The trunk and the roots can be more detailed, perhaps with some shading. Imagine that one side of the tree is in the sun—and hence, lighter—and that the other side is in shadow and should be painted with darker shades. Blend them together in the middle.

4 On your palette, put some different colored paints that match your leaf colors—you'll want at least a dark, medium, and light color. Dip a fluffy brush into your darkest color and then dab it on a paper towel to remove excess paint. Then dab the paintbrush repeatedly around the tree branches. Next, on top of the darkest paint, dab on some of your medium color. Be sure to leave some of the darker shade showing at the bottom and through some of your leaves. Lastly, use a bit of the light color as a highlight and dab it at the top of a few branches. Once dry, apply an acrylic sealer to the wood slice.

learn how to turn this painted wood slice into a wall hanging! Visit www. quartoknows.com/page/nature-art.

Leaf Study Garland

WITH ALLISON HETZELL

Enjoy a hike through nature, and collect some leaves to make a beautiful garland to hang in your home!

Materials
- 5 wood slices (about 3" across)
- 5 different leaves
- Drill
- Pencil and eraser
- Acrylic paint
- Paint palette
- Various paintbrushes
- Water and paper towel
- Acrylic sealer
- Hemp cord or twine

1 Head outdoors and collect at least five different types of leaves. If you won't be starting the project right away, press them between the pages of a book or under something flat and heavy to keep them from curling up. It's a good idea to keep them pressed flat in between the steps as well so that the leaves look the same as you continue to work on your project.

2

Take your five wood slices and drill a hole near the top of each, making sure to drill inside the wood and not the bark. Then sketch the outline of a different leaf onto each wood slice in pencil. Notice not only the shapes of the leaves but their edges and veins. Are the edges toothy or smooth? Do the veins slope evenly upward from the centers or branch out from other veins?

If your leaves have spotty areas, try watering down some of the paint in the correct color and dabbing it onto the appropriate area—it will be a lighter, more translucent color and spread out into a more organic shape.

3

Fill your paint palette with all the different colors you may use. Begin your paintings with a base layer on the leaves, using the most dominant colors to fill the leaves.

4

Start building up your paintings by using more specific colors and shading. When the underlying colors of the leaves are dry, use a small, thin paintbrush to add smaller details, such as leaf veins, spots, and toothier edges.

5

When the paintings are finished and completely dry, apply a coating of acrylic sealer to each wood slice to protect the painting. Cut a strand of hemp cord about 5 feet long. Using an overhand knot, make a loop at one end of the cord for hanging. Then string the first wood slice on and, about 4 inches from the end of the looped cord, tie a square knot above the wood slice and pull it tight. Repeat with the remaining wood slices, leaving about 4 inches between each knot. Finish by tying another loop at the other end of the cord and your garland is ready for display!

Woodburned Herb Rack

WITH ALLISON HETZELL

This is a beautiful piece for drying and displaying your favorite herbs from the garden! This woodburned drying rack is a great way to practice your pyrography skills and keep freshly dried herbs in your kitchen.

Materials
- Wood slice (around 8" wide)
- Pencil and eraser
- Woodburning tool*
- 5 screw-in cup hooks (1.25")
- Polyurethane sealer
- Sandpaper (220-grit)
- Sawtooth hanger and nails
- Hammer
- Hemp cord
- 5 fresh herbs of your choice
- Scissors

* Note: Woodburning tools are affordable and available at any art supply retailer.

1

With a pencil, mark five spots along the bottom of your wood slice for the hooks, beginning with the center and working out toward the sides. Each spot should be about 1½ inches apart. Be sure to mark the wood, not the bark.

2

Next draw your design, selecting five of your favorite herbs. It helps to practice on paper first, studying the leaf patterns of your herbs and practicing how you'd like to write the text. Write the word "Herbs" in large letters at the top, and then the name of an herb centered above each of the five marked spots at the bottom. Lastly, sketch the herbs above their corresponding names.

3

Select a writing tip for your woodburner. I use a small, ballpoint tip, but some woodburners come with tapered points or chisel tips that also work well for lettering. Once your chosen tip is attached, heat up the woodburner and trace the herb names and the word "Herbs."

4

Next woodburn your herb sketches, simply going over your pencil lines with the woodburner. I use a small knife tip to outline the herbs in thin, crisp lines, but a sharp-edged chisel tip would also work well. Tilt the woodburning pen and use the very end of the tip—the sharpest point—to do smaller, more detailed areas. When you're done, erase any visible pencil marks.

Don't panic if you make a mistake! Small mistakes and scorch marks can usually be removed with fine-grit sandpaper or a hobby knife.

5

With a soft brush, coat the edges and top of the wood slice with an even layer of sealer. Once dry, apply a layer on the back. After this first layer dries, lightly sand the front and back of the wood slice with fine-grit sandpaper (220-grit works well) to smooth. You don't want to sand down to the raw wood—just enough to remove any prickly areas. Dust off the wood slice and apply two more coats of sealer to get a nice, protective covering.

6

When the sealer is dry, attach a sawtooth hanger to the back of the wood slice. To do this, first mark the middle of the wood slice and center the hanger. Then use a hammer to lightly and carefully nail the hanger in place so you don't crack the wood. Then screw a cup hook in each of the marked spaces below the herb names.

Make sure the length of the screws and hanger aren't longer than the thickness of the wood slice, or they will poke through the opposite side.

7 Collect each of your herbs into a nice bundle and tightly wrap the ends in hemp cord, tying a square knot to secure. Leave about 8 inches of extra hemp cord on one end and tie an overhand knot with the extra cord, creating a loop at the end that you can use to hang the herbs to dry from their corresponding hooks.

Woodburned Constellation Coasters

WITH ALLISON HETZELL

Try out different woodburning tips, and get to know some constellations while making this fun set of stargazer coasters!

Materials
- 4 wood slices (around 3½"–4" across)
- Pencil and eraser
- Woodburning tool
- Sandpaper (220-grit) or a craft knife
- Polyurethane sealer
- Paintbrush
- Sheet of felt (9" x 12")
- Marker
- Scissors
- Craft or wood glue

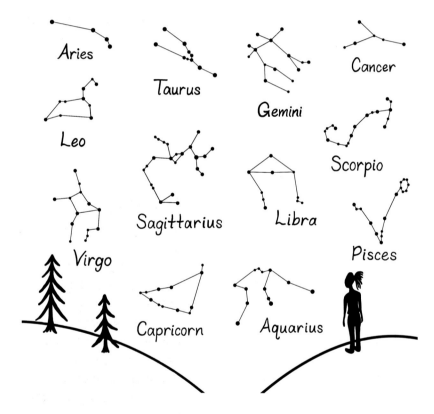

You can use my constellation references for your own coasters—or you can research other constellations to use.

1 Using the constellation of your choice, sketch a simple design of a stargazer on a hill onto each wood slice. Start with two sloping hills at the bottom—just two single lines with one disappearing behind the other. Next add a couple of pine trees on one hill and a silhouetted stick figure on the opposite hill. Draw the constellation centered in the sky above the hills; surround it with other stars, using dots, tiny circles, and diamonds.

You can use the same constellation on all of the wood slices or a different one on each. Try changing the number of trees and people too— or maybe even add a dog or a cat!

2

For the first part of the woodburning, select the tapered point or ballpoint tip for your woodburner. Once it's heated, trace the sketches of people, filling in each figure with a solid, dark burn so they look like silhouettes. Use this same technique to woodburn the trees, making the lines thick and dark so that they stand out. Finish by burning the dot- and circle-shaped stars.

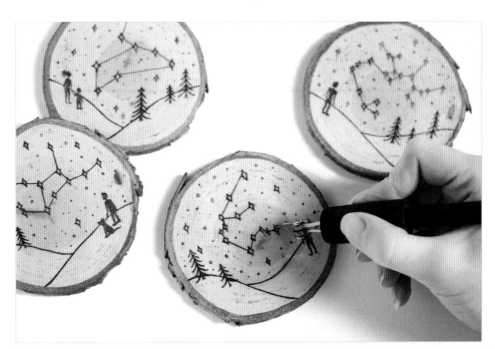

3

Next switch to a tapered chisel or knife tip on your woodburner to do some of the finer linework. Start by burning the two hill lines, skipping over the parts already burned with the trees and people. Then burn the diamond-shaped stars of your constellation and the lines that connect them.

Shading

To achieve nice, faded shading with a woodburner, start by setting your woodburning tip on the area that should be the darkest, and then drag it in the direction the shading should fade. The tip is the hottest when it first touches the wood, so the burn will be the darkest there. Moving the tip quickly will create a lighter, more even fade, since the woodburner won't have time to fully reheat. It's a good idea to practice your shading technique on a piece of scrap wood before trying on your actual project. But even if you make a mistake, sandpaper, a craft knife, and a little imagination can help fix it!

4

Switch to a shading tip for the last part of woodburning to add some color to the hills. Darken the bottom of each hill, as well as the area where the background hill disappears behind the foreground hill. To create a faded look, lightly drag your woodburning tip away from the darkest area. When you're finished, use fine-grit sandpaper or a craft knife to lighten any scorch marks or areas that are too dark.

5 Once your design is complete, use a paintbrush to apply a polyurethane sealer in an even layer, letting each coat dry completely in between. The sealer will make the coasters easier to clean and keep condensation out of the wood. Repeat for a total of three or four coats, or until the wood has a smooth, protective layer. Repeat for the bottom of the wood slices.

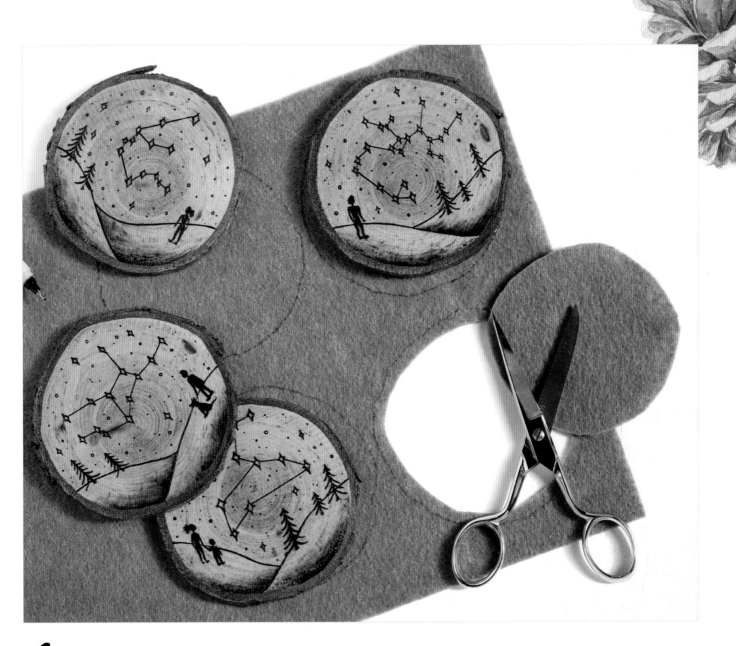

6 After the polyurethane is completely dry, take the sheet of felt and trace around each wood slice with a marker. Cut out each circle about a quarter of an inch within this line so that the felt won't be visible at the edges of the coasters.

7 Using craft or wood glue, attach the felt to the bottoms of your coasters. Make sure the glue reaches to the edges of the felt so they don't peel off, and be sure to press it down firmly.

8 Once the glue is dry, your coasters
are ready to use!

Woodburned Pieces & Color

WITH MONICA MOODY

This demonstration details a few ways to add color to woodburned art using FolkArt® antiquing medium and Inktense® pencils.

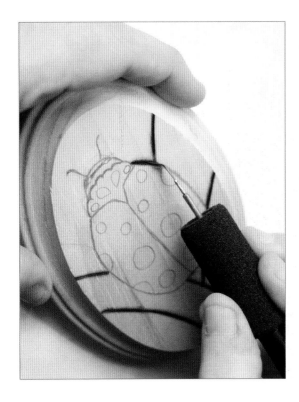

 Begin by sketching a ladybug and barn owl on two wooden oval plaques. Next burn in the outlines.

 Note the black item below the burner. A tip cleaner is a little tool for removing the carbon build-up from your woodburning pen tips.

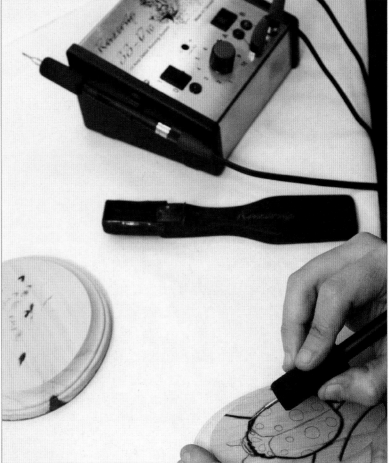

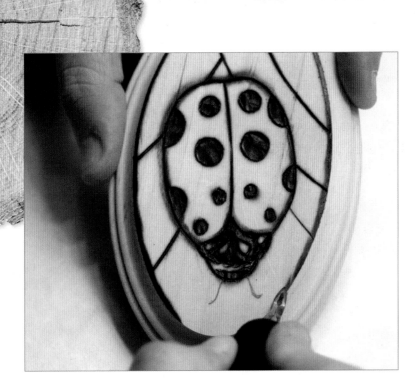

3

Burn a dark border on the top edges of the plaque using the triangle-shaped shader tip pen.

4

Use an extra-small skew for smaller lines and details.

5

Add a little shading with a triangle-shaped shader.

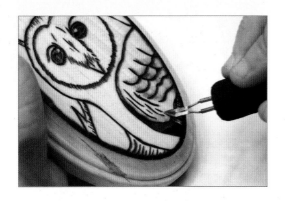

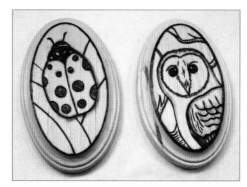

6 ⋘

Paint FolkArt® antiquing medium around the edges, and then quickly wipe it off with a paper towel.

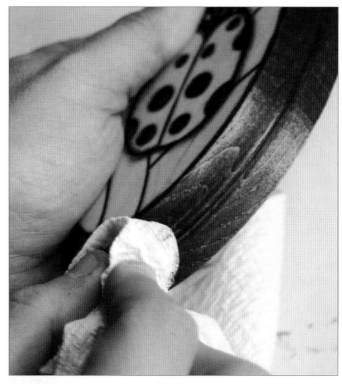

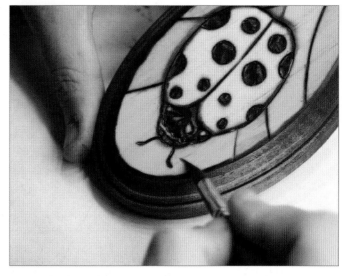

7 ⋘

Add color with Inktense pencils.

8 ⋘

Add water with a brush to the areas colored with Inktense pencils. The color will blend and become more vibrant.

9 ◄◄ Final touches: Use a white, oil-based, fine-tipped Sharpie® to add details to the ladybug and owl faces.

Two types of pens were used to burn these pieces: A triangle-shaped shader tip pen, turned on its side for lines and used flat for darkening solid areas (A), and an extra-small skew pen for thinner lines and details (B).

A   B

Wooden Wearables

WITH MONICA MOODY

Create woodburned pendants from slices of maple. The slices of maple have a very natural look, with the bark still on the outside edges. However, you could also make these pendants from laser-cut wooden circles or other shapes available from hobby stores.

1

Sand each slice on both sides, and drill a hole at the top with a Dremel® tool. Sketch designs onto the slice with a pencil.

2

Burn thicker lines with the side of the triangle-shaped shader tip pen, and use a small skew pen to burn smaller lines and details.

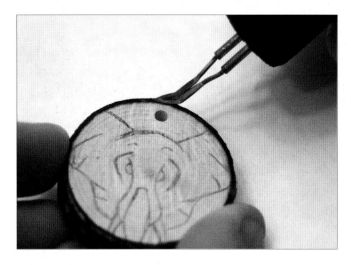

3

Use a triangle-shaped shader tip pen to burn a border on the bark around the top edge of the slice.

4

Use wood stain marker to color in the background.

With shorter cords, these pendants can become ornaments, which make great handmade holiday gifts. Wooden or colored beads also add a nice touch. Finish each pendant with a light coat or two of Polycrylic®.

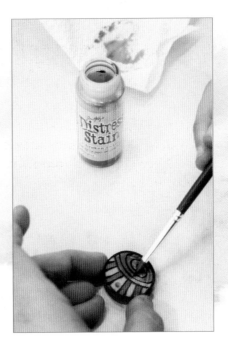

For this pendant, use a blue Tim Holtz® Distress Stain with a paintbrush.

5 String finished pendants with waxed thread. You could also use a chain or a leather or hemp cord.

OTHER NATURAL ELEMENTS

Painted Feather

WITH KATIE BROOKS

Painted feathers make a unique statement! The nature of the feather makes this a more challenging canvas, but don't let that intimidate you. Keep in mind that the feathers of many bird species are protected by federal law in the United States, so use discretion when collecting in the wild, or purchase your feathers from an art and craft supply store.

Materials
- Feathers
- Craft paints
- White acrylic paint
- Matte varnish (optional)
- Paintbrushes
- Paint

1

Coat both sides of the feather with a layer or two of white acrylic paint. Many feathers have a natural water-repellent coating to keep them dry; this coating could cause painting trouble if you don't create a base first.

2

Begin the sky with pale yellow, working out toward a strong yellow and soft orange. No harsh lines here—it's a cloudy day!

3

Continue bringing the sky's colors outward to the edge of the feather and horizon lines, and introduce a faded yellow-green from the horizon line down to begin the mountain range.

4

Begin creating the layers of the mountain range, darkening each line or mountain as you move forward in the scene.

5

Continue this process, using a slightly deeper green each time to create the effect of atmospheric perspective. Bring the front of the mountain range line all the way to the bottom edge of the feather with dark green, and check for any white space in the landscape that needs to be covered!

6

Lightly tap the surface with your smallest brush, loaded with your darkest green paint, to create foliage in the foreground.

8 Add some evergreen trees, painting a simple line for each tree and building out the foliage one side at a time, tapering toward the top. I depicted a tiny flock of birds migrating south for the winter in my landscape. Using natural elements in artwork means much more when you find inspiration there too! Seal your painting with a matte varnish when you're finished.

Painted Acorn

WITH KATIE BROOKS

Whimsical painted acorns are the perfect way to capture changing seasons. Make as many as you like—you could string them on some baker's twine to create a pretty garland or group some together in a small dish. You can even make a pendant with the finished acorn!

Materials
- Acorn (Choose a large acorn free of holes, which could cause decay after sealing)
- Glue
- Craft paints
- Gloss varnish
- Round, fine-tipped paintbrushes
- Paint palette

1  Gently remove the acorn's cap and set it aside. We'll reattach it later!

2  Using a warm yellow, begin scattering the leaf shape of your choice around the acorn, leaving plenty of room for leaves of other colors! I chose a ginkgo leaf, because they turn a lovely, bold yellow in autumn!

3 With a muted orange, begin adding different leaves among the yellow leaves. Leave room for one more leaf variety. I recommend making these a bit smaller than the yellow leaves. Varying sizes add visual interest!

4

Choose a third unique leaf shape and add it with burgundy-red in the remaining spaces. At this point, the leaves should be evenly spaced, with no jarring gaps between. If you find a gap that's too large, simply fill it with another leaf!

5

With a bit of dark brown on your smallest brush, add a few lines to each leaf to suggest its stem and veins. Don't worry too much about making this perfect, just try to capture the impression.

You'll likely need to apply multiple coats of paint for each leaf, depending on the thickness of your paint.

6

With a small dip of white paint on your smallest brush, accent the spaces between the leaves with tiny dots. Cover the acorn with a few coats of gloss varnish to bring out the colors and protect the finished painting. Then align and reattach the cap with the strong glue of your choice.

NATURE-INSPIRED ART

Screen-Printed Pop Art

WITH CHELSEA FOY

This nature-inspired, screen-printed pop art project is such a cool and unexpected way to add a little art to your walls! Screen printing may seem like a difficult or advanced skill, but it's actually pretty simple. Once you give it a try, you'll be screen printing everything you own!

Materials
- Blank stretched canvas
- Craft paint
- Liquid gilding
- Mod Podge®
- Small paintbrushes
- 2 small foam paintbrushes
- Computer and printer
- Permanent marker
- Scissors
- Embroidery hoop
- Sheer fabric
- Washi tape (optional)

1  Stretch the sheer fabric across the embroidery hoop and secure it with the inner hoop, pulling taut on all sides to ensure there are no wrinkles. Trim around the edges of the fabric to clear away the excess.

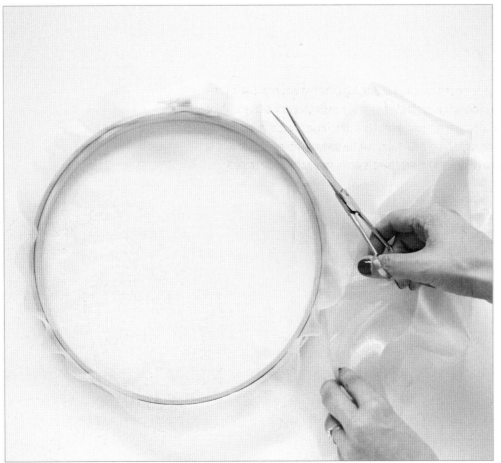

2 Find an image of a plant or other natural object to screen print. Black-and-white, high-contrast images that consist of simple shapes work best. Print the image on white paper. Then place the fabric hoop over the printed image. Trace the image lightly onto the fabric with a permanent marker. Be sure to trace along all edges—anywhere there is white space should be traced!

3 Using a variety of small paintbrushes, apply Mod Podge over all the *negative space*—anywhere there is white on the printed image. Let dry, and then apply a second coat of Mod Podge over the first layer.

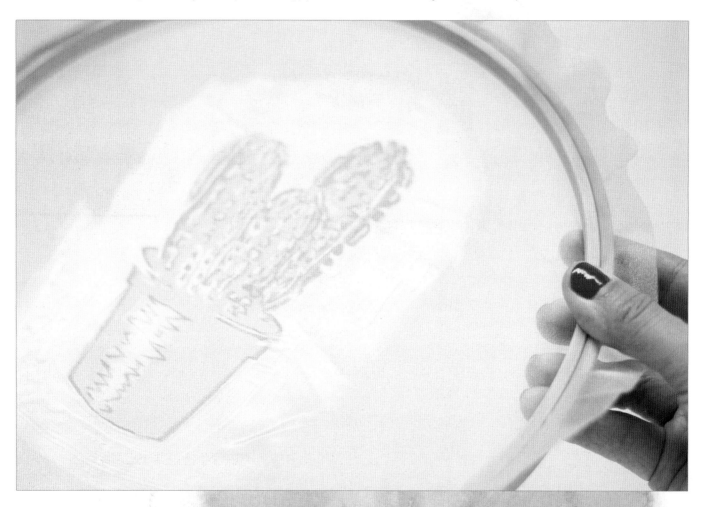

4

If you'd like to map out where the images will be screen printed, create a grid on the canvas using washi tape.

5

Carefully screen on the images. Set the hoop over the spot where you want the image to appear. Load a small foam brush with a good amount of craft paint. Being careful not to let the hoop move, press paint over the image firmly. Add paint until the entire image is covered. Gently pull away the screen, and you should have a screen-printed version of your image.

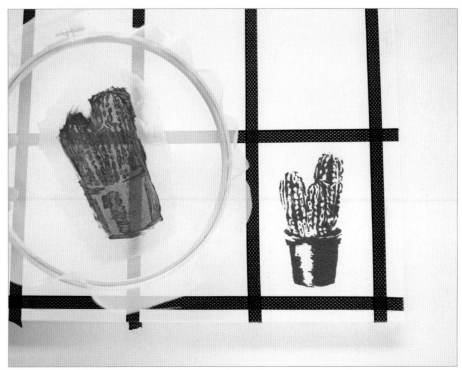

You may find that it works better to apply the paint in strokes rather than pressing it in. Experiment first on a piece of paper to see which technique works best for you.

Repeat the process until you have filled the canvas with the image. Allow the canvas to dry completely.

7

Choose a few spots to add a little gold. Once the canvas is dry, set the screen down again on one of the images and brush on a bit of liquid gilding with a new foam brush. Don't cover the entire screen; apply only to about half of the image. Pull the screen carefully away.

118

8  Allow the gilding to dry completely. Then put up your new pop art and admire!

Golden Moth

WITH GABRI JOY KIRKENDALL

I love finding ways to layer gouache over watercolor for stunning effects, especially when using gold metallic gouache paint, which creates a foil effect. A golden moth makes the perfect subject for combining these mediums.

Materials
- Watercolor paper
- Watercolor paints
- Metallic gouache
- Paintbrushes

1 Begin by sketching the shape of the moth. Then use watercolor paint to begin. I chose a beautiful sunset palette to complement the gold gouache. I paint the top of the top wings a light yellow and add an orange stroke along the bottom while the paint is wet to allow the colors to blend.

2 Allow the paint to dry. Then paint the bottom wings in the same manner. I use light pink and dark pink. Add feather antennae at the top with less diluted yellow paint. Let the paint dry.

3 Pull out the metallic gouache and begin to paint, working from the outside in. I start by painting the edges of the moth first. Then I begin filling the wings with pretty designs.

If you use too much water with metallic gouache the paint may separate.

4 Finish painting the gouache pattern. I only add a few simple details to the bottom wings, allowing the top wings to take center stage. Let the gouache dry completely, and then step back and enjoy the effect!

Gouache Feather Illustration

WITH GABRI JOY KIRKENDALL

Gouache lends beautiful contrast to artwork, and it is also perfect for adding patterns and details on watercolor. Just remember to use a fine-tipped brush for smaller details!

Materials
- Watercolor paper
- Pencil
- Watercolor paints
- White gouache
- Paintbrushes

1

First sketch the outline of the feathers. Then paint inside the outline first with water, which will help the watercolor paint blend well. While the paper is damp, begin adding color.

2

Continue adding color, painting wet-into-wet to keep the colors blending smoothly together.

3

Repeat the process to paint the second feather. Let the feathers dry, and then letter a message in the middle. If you're not comfortable with lettering, you could also draw and paint a third feather in the middle.

YOU DESERVE

magic

4 Use white gouache to add detail and pattern to the feathers. The effect is beautiful!

Watercolor Raindrops

Materials
- Watercolor paper
- Pencil and eraser
- Watercolor paints
- Paintbrush

WITH GABRI JOY KIRKENDALL

A great way to practice technique—and create some cool patterned art at the same time—is to use a favorite shape. I picked raindrops because they remind me of the cool, damp weather of my beautiful Pacific Northwest, with one tiny drop hinting at the promise of warmer days.

1 Use a pencil to sketch light, straight, evenly spaced lines on watercolor paper. Then begin to paint each shape, keeping the spacing between each one even. On some of my raindrops I use an even layer of color; on others I paint a lighter background and then drop in darker bits of paint to create a cool feathered effect.

2

Keep working to fill each row with evenly spaced shapes. I used a combination of cobalt, ultramarine, and black to paint my raindrops.

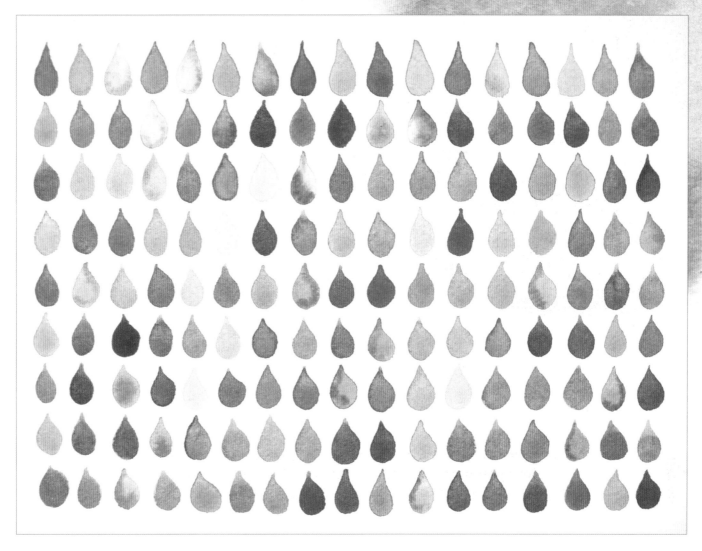

3 Choose one shape to paint a different color. I used a bright, sunny peach color on a solitary drop. Paint the rest of the shapes in the same colors. Let the paint dry, and then erase the pencil lines!

Floral Watercolor

WITH GABRI JOY KIRKENDALL

Materials
• Watercolor paper
• Watercolor paints
• Metallic gouache
• Paintbrushes

There is nothing so classic and beautiful as flowers, and the history of art is overgrown with floral still life! I prefer a more abstract representation, rather than pure realism. A pretty floral piece can stand alone or provide a beautiful background for another project.

1

Begin by selecting the flower and colors you wish to paint. I chose roses in shades of pink and champagne and used a feathered brushstroke followed by a darker color on the inside of each petal to create depth.

2

Next begin painting leaves. I start with larger, brighter leaves close to the roses, framing them. First I paint the outline and fill it in with paint. Then, before the paint dries, I add stripes in a darker shade to simulate the folded nature of the leaves.

3

Continue adding leaves. I used a darker shade with a little more blue to paint smaller background leaves to complete the frame.

4

Just for fun, use gold metallic gouache to add some dots as an accent to finish the illustration.

Also available from Walter Foster Publishing

978-1-63322-481-0

978-1-63322-378-3

978-1-63322-241-0

978-1-63322-484-1

978-1-63322-216-8

978-1-63322-048-5

978-1-63322-072-0

Visit www.QuartoKnows.com